Chance of a Lifetime

MARGARET IGGULDEN and JULIA ALLEN

Level 3

Series Editors: Andy Hopkins and Jocelyn Potter

Pearson Education Limited
Edinburgh Gate, Harlow,
Essex CM20 2JE, England
and Associated Companies throughout the world.

ISBN 0 582 42748 7

This edition first published 2000

NEW EDITION

Copyright © Penguin Books Ltd 2000
Illustrations by Phil Bannister
Cover design by Bender Richardson White

Typeset by Bender Richardson White
Set in 11/14pt Bembo
Printed and bound in Denmark by Norhaven A/S, Viborg

*All rights reserved; no part of this publication may be reproduced, stored
in a retrieval system, or transmitted in any form or by any means,
electronic, mechanical, photocopying, recording or otherwise, without the
prior written permission of the Publishers.*

Published by Pearson Education Limited in association with
Penguin Books Ltd, both companies being subsidiaries of Pearson Plc

---

For a complete list of the titles available in the Penguin Readers series please write to your local
Pearson Education office or to: Marketing Department, Penguin Longman Publishing,
5 Bentinck Street, London W1M 5RN.

Contents

		page
Introduction		v
Chapter 1	The Phone Call	1
Chapter 2	A Day at the Beach	4
Chapter 3	The Astrologer	8
Chapter 4	The Tour Group	12
Chapter 5	At the Hotel	14
Chapter 6	At the Louvre	17
Chapter 7	Into Switzerland	20
Chapter 8	In Basle	22
Chapter 9	Karen Arrives	23
Chapter 10	An Accident at the Lake	25
Chapter 11	From Venice to Rome	29
Chapter 12	On the Road Again	34
Chapter 13	From Italy to Greece	35
Chapter 14	An Evening at the Theatre	40
Chapter 15	Istanbul	43
Chapter 16	Holiday Photos	48
Chapter 17	At the Airport	49
Chapter 18	Helen's Decision	53
Activities		56

Introduction

The astrologer smiled. 'Now, let's see what's going to happen in the next few months. Hmm. You're going to travel and meet new people.'
  'Yes! I've got a job as a tour guide.'
  'But Pluto is here. Pluto means secrets. Dark secrets. Deep secrets.'
  'Secrets? My secrets?'
  'I don't know. But be careful. Perhaps secret things will happen.'
  'A secret love?'
  'I don't know. It's too difficult to say . . .'

When Helen travels through Europe, on her first job after university, she starts to discover important things. What does she learn? Something about herself? Or about the other people on the trip? What secrets are they hiding? And what will Helen's future be?

Margaret Iggulden has her own English Language Homestay Company. She has lived and taught in Papua New Guinea, Kenya and Kuwait. Julia Allen is a writer and an artist. She lived in the Middle East and East Africa as a child, and since then she has travelled in the western states of the USA.
  Margaret and Julia began writing together in 1986.
  Some other stories by them are: *African Adventure* (1988), *The Sacrifice* (1989), *Who Wants to be a Star* (1989), *Susan and The Flying Saucer* (1990), *The Bongey Bees* (1998) and *Save Our Wood* (1999). This story was written specially for Penguin Readers.

Chapter 1 The Phone Call

Helen couldn't sleep. She opened her eyes and looked at her watch. It was three o'clock. She switched on the small light above her bed and read the letter again.

Dear Ms Davies,

  Thank you for coming to see us. As we told you, we need a tour guide for a trip from London to Istanbul. We would like to offer you this job . . .

Helen stopped reading. 'What should I do? I need to talk to Tom about it,' she thought.

She looked at Tom's photograph on the table next to her. It showed a tall, dark-haired young man with a beard. The photograph was taken just after their final examinations at Swansea University.

'I remember that day,' she thought. 'We drove to a beach and went for a long walk. It was a perfect day – and only a month ago.

'Oh, Tom. What are we going to do? You never wanted to talk about us! And now you're in Scotland and I'm in Wales. Oh, why aren't you here?'

Helen got out of bed and went to the window. She stood there, thinking. Penarth was still asleep. The town was silent.

'I can speak French and Italian. People tell me I'm intelligent and pretty. What am I afraid of? The job won't be very difficult. It's a wonderful chance to travel and see more of Europe! Italy! Greece! Turkey! I can't stay here in Penarth. But . . .'

She went back to the table by the bed and looked at the photograph again. She loved Tom. She was sure.

'But does he really love me? He's only phoned once since that wonderful day on the beach. Perhaps he's waiting to get a job. Then, perhaps he'll ask me to marry him. Perhaps . . . '

She lay down on the bed again but couldn't stop thinking. Did she really want to take twelve people across Europe in a small bus?

'Perhaps it'll be fun. Or perhaps it'll be terrible. And can I really do a job like that? There'll be all kinds of different people and different nationalities. Perhaps my friend Jill can help me. I'll go and see her next Thursday. Perhaps . . . '

At last she fell asleep.

♦

She was in Africa. A man was pointing a gun at her. She was trying to stop him killing a wild animal.

'Helen! There's a phone call for you!'

Helen woke up from her dream. Her mother was standing next to her bed.

'It's Tom. He's phoning from Scotland!' she said.

Helen got out of bed, and ran downstairs. She was still dreaming about Africa when she picked up the phone.

'Helen! I've got good news. A big international company has offered me a job!'

'That's wonderful, Tom! I'm so happy for you. When do you start? Is the job in Scotland?'

Helen waited for his answer. Perhaps now he wanted her to marry him. There was a short silence.

'No, the job isn't in Scotland,' he said finally.

'Not in Scotland?'

There was another silence. Helen knew something was wrong. Tom was usually quick to tell her everything about himself and his plans.

'No, Helen. This company is all over the world. They . . . ' He began to speak very quickly. 'They want me to go to Australia.'

Helen was very surprised. She was trying to think – to understand. But she couldn't.

'Australia?'

'Yes, they want me to go to Brisbane. Immediately! I'm going to study the use of the sun's heat to warm houses and factories! I have to go to London tomorrow to get a passport! I'm leaving on Saturday.'

'Saturday? Will . . . Will I see you before you go?' Helen asked. She tried to sound calm. 'Isn't he even going to ask me about my plans?' she thought. 'Shall I tell him about my job with Global Tours?'

'Er – no – well – I must go now. I've got a lot of things to do before I go and . . . ' She waited. 'I'm sorry,' he said.

Again, there was silence.

Helen suddenly realized two things. Tom didn't want to see her, and he wasn't in love with her. She was nearly in tears, but she fought them.

'I've got a job, too. I wanted to talk to you about it. But you're too busy. I'll talk to Jill about it.'

'Yes, Jill's great. She's a good friend. You should phone her. She'll listen. So . . . '

He didn't even ask about the job. Helen waited before she spoke. 'Well, Tom, I hope you have a great life out in Australia. Write or phone, when you have time.'

'Helen . . . '

'I'm sure you'll have a wonderful time. Goodbye, Tom.'

She went back to her room and threw herself on her bed. 'Tom and I had fun at university,' she thought. 'But now university's finished and we're history. That's it.'

She began to cry.

Chapter 2   A Day at the Beach

A few days later, Helen caught a bus to Swansea to see Jill. It was the holidays but her friend was still at the university. Jill was studying trees. She wanted to work abroad, but first she had to finish her studies.

It was a sunny day and they decided to go for a walk along the beach. They took off their shoes and walked by the water.

Jill looked at her friend. 'You don't seem very happy, Helen.'

'I've got no job and no money. I'm living in Penarth with my mother, and Tom is flying to Australia today. He didn't even want to see me.'

'You're really unhappy about Tom, aren't you?'

'Yes,' Helen replied. 'Jill, I need to ask you something. It's about going to Australia. Shall I go and look for a job near him?'

'Run after him, you mean?'

'Er – no. Not exactly.'

Jill looked at Helen. It was a long, hard look.

'Oh, it looks like that, doesn't it?' Helen said quickly.

'Yes,' Jill answered. 'You know I've always been honest with you, Helen.'

Helen picked up a large white stone and threw it into the sea.

'Let's look at you,' Jill said. 'You can speak French and Italian. You're very intelligent. You have lovely fair hair, blue eyes and a pretty face. You're also a good friend. You're – usually – happy, and you love life.'

'Well . . . '

'But you just want a boyfriend.'

'Yes, you're right.' Helen kicked at the sand. Some sea birds suddenly flew up from the rocks. 'But don't all women think about boyfriends?'

'Helen, we're young. We're intelligent. Life is more than marriage and children. Perhaps you should think about yourself. Who is Helen? I think she's a great woman.'

Helen was silent for a few minutes. The sea birds cried above them. The sun disappeared behind some clouds, and the sky looked grey and dark.

'But I want to have a husband – and a family. Well, I think I do.'

'But Helen, have you ever really thought about it? Marriage and children aren't everything. You can use your languages, and get a good job. You give everything to your boyfriends, and they don't give anything to you. They take from you. They don't respect you. You're not going to like this . . . ' Jill stopped.

'I want to know, Jill. Tell me.'

'You're their mother.'

'Their *mother*?' Helen screamed.

Jill took Helen by the hand and danced around the beach with her.

'Mum! Mum!' she shouted. She wanted Helen to laugh.

Then Helen smiled. 'I'm not, Jill. That's not true.'

'Yes it is. Look at you and Tom. You cooked his meals, you washed his clothes, you did his shopping. You listened to his problems. That's exactly what his mother does. Be yourself, Helen.'

'Myself? I thought I was.' Helen pushed her long fair hair away from her face. There was a strong wind now. '*You* have a boyfriend!' She was feeling sorry for herself, and she was also beginning to feel quite angry with Jill.

'But I don't give all my time to him. I'm not always there when he needs me. Not all the time. I need time for myself. I don't cook him beautiful meals. I tell him to cook for me!'

Helen smiled. 'Oh, yes, I remember! What a dinner! Boiled eggs, boiled vegetables and half-cooked rice! Ergh!'

They both laughed.

'The world is changing, Helen. It needs women who are strong and independent. It needs women who have careers. We can change the world. We *must* change the world!'

'Yes, you're right.' Helen thought for a second and then turned to Jill. 'Are you angry with men?'

'Angry? No, I'm not angry with men. But they're not going to decide what I should do.'

'What do you think I should do, Jill?'

'Why not take this job? You speak French and Italian perfectly. You're good at making friends with people.'

'I'll be a good tour guide, won't I?'

'Yes!' Jill looked at her. 'Why don't you go to an astrologer?'

'An astrologer? Do you believe in astrology, Jill?' Helen asked.

'Well . . . I went to an astrologer once, and she did a chart for me. She's very good. I found out a lot about myself from her. If you see her, perhaps you'll find out something about yourself and your future.'

'OK. Why not!' Helen agreed. She felt happier.

'I've got a present for you.' Jill gave her a brightly-coloured packet.

Helen carefully took the coloured paper off. It was a plate, with some writing on it.

'Read it!' Jill said, smiling happily.

'"Be true to yourself",' Helen read.

She looked at her friend, and they both smiled.

Chapter 3   The Astrologer

Helen took her diary from the table next to her bed. She began to write.

July 9th
Dear Diary,
I'm glad I went to see Jill. But I don't agree with everything that she said. Tom hasn't phoned me, but he has phoned his mother. She rang and told me. I felt very hurt. I miss him.

But I've decided to take the job with Global Tours. So I'll be a tour guide. I'm going to take twelve people, between eighteen and forty, around Europe. Who knows? Perhaps I'll meet an interesting man and live in a big house in Italy. Oops! I mustn't let Jill read this diary!

I'm not going to think about Tom! I'm not!

July 10th
Tom still hasn't written. Shall I phone his mother? Why not?
Later:
Why did I do that? Why did I ring? I'm even more unhappy now. Tom has phoned her twice. Twice! But no call for me! He's living in a wonderful flat in Brisbane and has already made some friends. Perhaps he's found a new girlfriend, too.

I think I'll go to that astrologer on Monday.

♦

A few days later, Helen knocked on the door of a small house in a dark, narrow street. The sign on the door said *Lisa Collins. Astrologer.*

Helen imagined Lisa. 'She'll have long black hair, and a lot of gold or silver, and brightly-coloured clothes.'

A woman of about thirty-five came to the door, wearing jeans and a blue shirt. And she wasn't wearing any gold or silver.

'Hi. I'm Lisa. Come in. Would you like a cup of tea?'

Helen looked around the flat before she sat down. It was large, with a lot of space.

Lisa gave her a cup with *Sagittarius* on it.

'Thank you for sending me your birth date: December the sixth. You're a Sagittarius. You like fun and parties and being with people,' Lisa said.

'That's true,' Helen answered. She began to feel calmer. Lisa was a nice woman.

Then Lisa showed Helen her astrology chart. 'You're the only person with a chart like this. Every person is completely different,' she explained.

Helen listened carefully when Lisa started talking about different planets: Venus, Mars, Uranus, Jupiter.

'Now, let's see: you've got Venus in Scorpio.'

'Is that bad?'

'Nothing is good or bad. It just means that you've got problems. With boyfriends! You always choose the wrong man. You choose the same kind every time. Proud men, full of their own importance. Men with secrets.'

Helen looked hard at the astrologer. 'Yes, you're right. But what can I do about it?'

'Be more careful. Try to understand what you're doing. You can solve the problem, but it won't be easy.'

'Oh,' Helen said. She didn't like what Lisa was telling her.

'Don't worry. You'll be all right.' The astrologer smiled. 'Now,

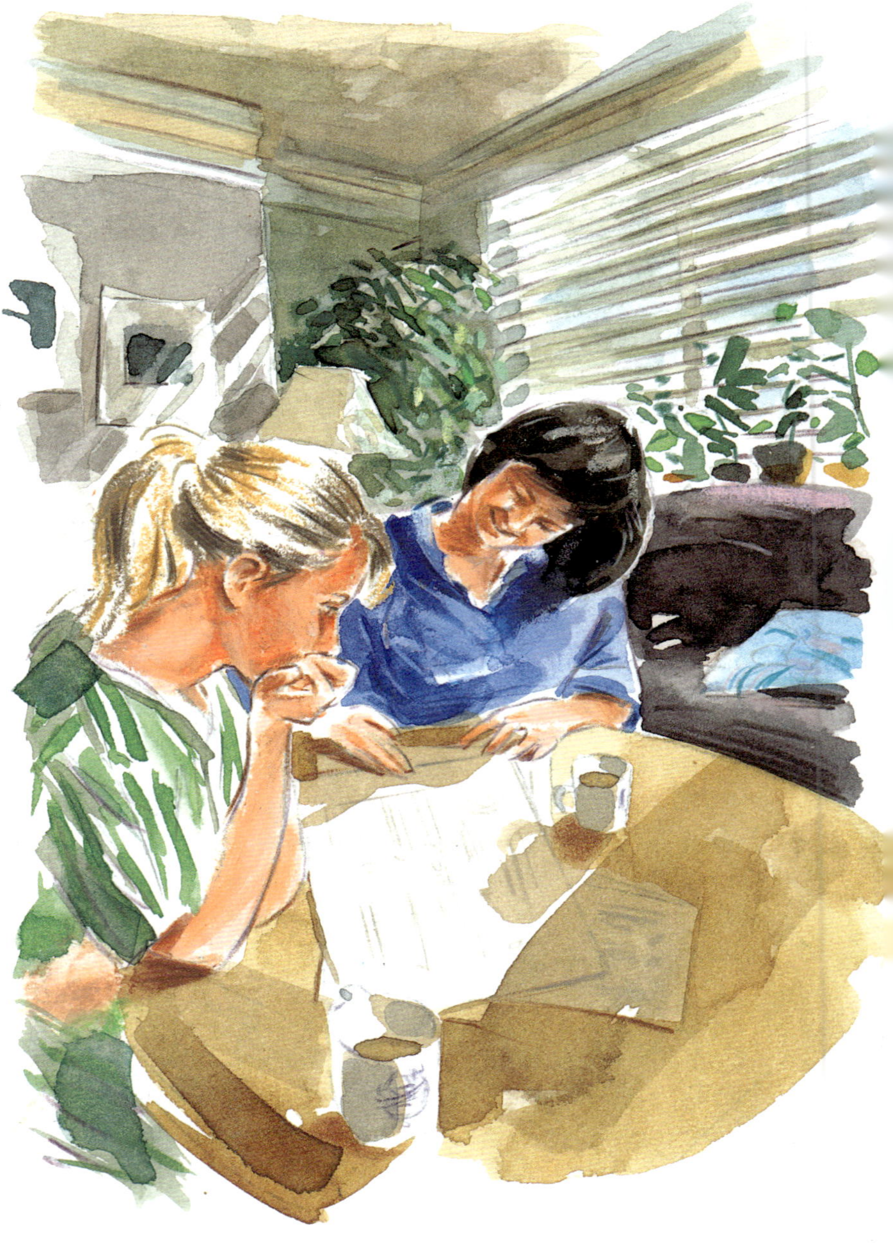

let's see what's going to happen in the next few months. Hmm. You're going to travel and meet new people.'

'Yes! I've got a job as a tour guide.'

'But Pluto is here. Pluto means secrets. Dark secrets. Deep secrets.'

'Secrets? My secrets?'

'I don't know. But be careful. Perhaps secret things will happen.'

'A secret love?'

'I don't know. It's too difficult to say exactly. But it's going to be a good time for you in many ways. You'll learn something important about yourself and your feelings.'

'Can you tell me more?'

'Yes,' Lisa said. 'You like travelling, so I'd like to draw another chart for you. This will be a map of the world at the time when you were born. It will show where all the planets were at exactly that minute. For example, if your Jupiter line goes through Russia, perhaps you'll have good luck in Russia.'

'I'm not really sure what she means by a "Jupiter line",' thought Helen. 'Is there a "Venus line"? Venus means love. Perhaps my Venus line goes through Greece and Turkey, or Italy. Will I find love there?'

Before Helen could ask about Venus, Lisa suddenly said, 'I want to tell you something important! You'll get your chance of a lifetime this year.'

'My chance of a lifetime?' Helen repeated.

'Yes, the thing that you really want to happen. It will change your life.'

'Really? That's wonderful. Maybe I'll find a good-looking boyfriend.' Helen was excited.

Lisa looked at her for a long time. 'Is that what you want?'

♦

July 18th
Dear Diary,

Tom went to Australia three weeks ago. I wait for the postman every day and listen for the phone, but there's nothing. Well – I must just forget him!

Perhaps Jill's right: there's more to life than a boyfriend. But all my school friends here in Penarth are married. I'm lonely. Very lonely. I need to have friends around me.

July 30th

A letter from Global Tours! I'm going to London on Saturday for a week's course. Then on 15th August the tour starts.

Still nothing from Tom. Mrs Jones at the post office told me to be very careful when I go to Europe. She thinks it's a dangerous place. Some people have a wonderful imagination!

Lisa has sent me my special world chart. It looks very interesting. I must study it when I have more time. I'm still worried about my new job. Will I be a good tour guide? I hope so. Perhaps this is my chance of a lifetime.

Chapter 4   The Tour Group

On 15th August, Helen walked into the offices of Global Tours in central London. She had her suitcase and a camera with her. A group of people was already sitting in the main room.

'This is my group,' she thought.

She looked again at the list. There were twelve names on it: six men and six women. The list had information about all of them, with their ages.

She began to compare the people in the room with the information on the list. There was a young woman in very expensive clothes. She looked bored and had a very big suitcase.

'Is there room for that in the bus?' Helen asked herself. She was beginning to worry already. She looked at the list again. 'Yes, that's probably Angela James, twenty-one. Hmm. Shall I say something to her about that case? No, not yet. I want her to like me.'

There were also two Americans on the list.

'Dr Bill Berryman and his wife, Maisie. That's useful; perhaps we'll need a doctor. But where are they? Are they the two over there, in bright yellow shirts? Ugh!'

Helen stopped herself. She didn't want to have a bad opinion of anyone in the group.

She noticed a woman with thick glasses and dark clothes. One of the names on the list was 'Mary Foxley. Thirty-two. Secretary'. 'Perhaps that's her,' Helen thought. 'She looks like a secretary. She's already writing postcards. And we haven't gone anywhere yet!'

There was also a very beautiful woman with short dark hair. She was wearing jeans and a red T-shirt, and reading a book – Sarah Lawrence, thirty? Helen looked around and saw another husband and wife, Tony and Jean Summers. He was wearing a business suit!

Three young men were smoking. They looked like university friends, and were probably Noel, Martin and Richard.

'I hope they don't smoke on the bus,' Helen thought.

And then there was a tall young man with fair hair and a beard, perhaps Vic Watson, twenty-four.

Helen looked at the list and then at the people again. Suddenly, she noticed something. There were twelve names on the list, but there were only eleven people in the office.

'Who's missing? Ah ... Karen Benton! The list says she'll meet us in Paris,' she thought.

Someone touched Helen on the shoulder. 'Hello, Helen. I'm Ben, driver number one, and this is Stan, driver number two. This is going to be a great trip.'

Helen looked at them and immediately felt good. They both looked friendly, and old enough to be her father.

'It's nice to meet you. I'm going to say hello to the group. Then we can start.'

'Fine, Helen. You're the boss,' said Stan, and picked up her case.

Helen was surprised. She *was* the boss. Suddenly she was frightened.

'I can do it, I can do it,' she said to herself.

She breathed in and out slowly, and walked to the middle of the office.

'Good morning, everyone. I'm Helen, your tour guide.' She looked at the group and smiled. 'I'm sure you're going to have a wonderful time. I'm here to help you with anything.'

'Anything?' the tall, fair-haired man asked. He smiled. Helen noticed that Angela, the girl with the big suitcase, seemed very interested in him.

She tried to remember the lessons from her course: 'Don't show your feelings. Be nice to the tourists. Make them happy.' She smiled politely and said, 'We're leaving in a few minutes. Another person is waiting for us in Paris, our first stop. Now, can I see your tickets and passports, please?'

Chapter 5 At the Hotel

Helen walked into the Hotel Britannia in Paris. The others were getting out of the bus. It was still only the first day, but already the American doctor, Bill Berryman, was angry. Noel wanted to smoke all the time.

Angela James added to the problem. 'I don't want to die of a terrible illness!' she said loudly. 'The smell is so bad too. Ugh!'

Most of the time Angela looked very bored. She only looked

excited when she was talking to Vic Watson.

'Yes,' Helen thought, 'he *is* good-looking.'

The man behind the hotel desk looked at her. She felt nervous, but she took a deep breath and introduced herself.

The man smiled and told her about the rooms. 'Your twelfth tourist, Karen Benton, will arrive tomorrow,' he said.

Helen thanked him and turned to tell the group about their rooms. There were rooms with double beds for the married people. She was the only person who had a single room. The others all had rooms with two single beds.

'Let's see. Angela and Mary are in Room—'

'Pardon?' Helen looked up from her list. 'I need a single room,' Angela said. 'I told Global Tours.'

'I'm afraid—' Helen began.

'I must have a single room.' Angela looked at Helen. There was silence.

Helen looked at her list again and took a deep breath. This was her first test. She felt angry. She knew she mustn't show it. 'I'll talk to the others first and then come back to you, Angela.'

Helen put Vic with Martin, and Sarah with Mary Foxley. Then she remembered. Karen Benton wasn't coming until the next day. So there was a room for Angela. The others took their bags and went to their rooms.

'There is a room that you can be alone in tonight, Angela. Karen hasn't arrived yet.'

'I want a single room *every* night.'

Helen hated the way that Angela spoke to her. What should she do?

'I'll phone Global Tours tomorrow morning and check your request with them. They didn't tell me about it.'

Angela put her hands in her pockets. 'Well, perhaps *I* didn't ask. I think my father did.'

Helen spoke quietly. 'Perhaps your father *didn't* ask, Angela. And we can't change everything now. I'm sure you understand that. I can't phone all the hotels in all the countries and ask for a single room for you.'

Angela looked at her. 'I can have your room, can't I, Helen?'

Helen could feel herself getting more and more angry. 'Shall I give her my room?' she thought. 'It will keep her quiet.'

Then she saw Ben looking at her from the bottom of the stairs.

'I'm afraid that's not possible, Angela,' Ben said. 'It's a company rule. The tour guide must have a single room. For a number of reasons.'

Angela looked at Ben and then back at Helen. 'Oh, really?' she said. Stan was standing by the desk and she turned to him. 'Pick up my case, will you? It's too heavy for me.'

Stan looked at her and his face went red. 'I don't– '

Just then, Vic walked across the room. He smiled at Helen and picked up Angela's case. 'Angela! What have you got in here? Rocks?'

They walked upstairs laughing.

Stan hit his hand on the desk. 'What a terrible woman! You were wonderful, Helen. I hope she gets better. She can't get worse. I don't like her at all.'

'It's been a long day,' said Helen. 'We must all get some sleep. It's going to be a busy day tomorrow.'

Chapter 6 At the Louvre

The group was standing in front of the Louvre★. Helen told them about it. It was opened in 1793, and it took two hours to walk through all the rooms.

Then they all stood and looked at the glass building in front of the museum.

Bill Berryman walked around it with his video camera.

'I want to show the people back in the States this wonderful building.'

'Well, I think it's stupid,' Angela said loudly. 'I can't understand why the French built it. And I can't understand how anyone can like it. Can you, Vic?'

★ Louvre: a famous museum of great paintings in Paris. One of its most famous paintings is the *Mona Lisa*.

Vic looked at Helen and said, 'It's a pity that it hasn't got water in it. I'd love to swim in it!'

Angela laughed. Helen looked at her. This young girl was rude to everyone. Nobody liked her. Nobody except Vic. He seemed to enjoy talking to her. Bill came over to talk to Helen.

'Can't you do something about her, Helen? This is a holiday, not a school trip for girls who haven't grown up yet.'

Helen looked at Angela again. Perhaps she should speak to her now.

'OK,' she told everyone. 'You've got two hours here. Then after lunch we're visiting Versailles★. I'll try to speak to Angela now.'

'Are you coming round the museum?' asked Mary. Mary tried to be friendly with everyone in the group, but nobody except Helen ever showed any interest in her.

'I've just got to talk to Angela about something, Mary. I'll join you later.'

Helen saw Angela and Vic walking towards the museum entrance.

'Angela, can I speak to you for a minute?' she called.

Angela looked angrily at Helen and then turned back to Vic.

'I'll wait for you inside, Angela,' Vic said, and smiled at Helen.

'Yes?' Angela stood with her hands in her pockets.

Helen took a deep breath. She didn't like this part of the job.

'Angela, we haven't begun very well. This is a holiday . . . ' Angela looked bored. 'I'm afraid that you're making people unhappy on this trip. Everyone wants to enjoy themselves and you're being – well – difficult.'

'You're just like one of my old teachers that taught me history. You never stop.'

'Angela, I want to be your friend. We all want to be friends and have a good time.'

'You're angry because Vic likes me and not you. You like him. I know. I can see it.' Angela turned and started to walk away.

Helen went red. 'Is she right?' she thought. 'Do I like Vic a lot?'

Helen looked at the glass building. There were lots of people around. They were talking and laughing. They were eating and taking photographs. Bill was still videoing the outside of the museum.

'Yes, I like Vic, but I'm still in love with Tom. Angela's just being stupid,' she decided.

★Versailles: a great palace outside Paris.

'Come on, Helen. Come and see the *Mona Lisa*,' Jean Summers shouted.

'Forget Angela. We'll throw her in a lake at Versailles and teach her to be polite!' laughed Tony, her husband.

Helen smiled at them. But she felt that Angela was still a problem.

Chapter 7 Into Switzerland

It was nine o'clock at night and Stan was driving the bus across France. Helen was still not exactly sure where Karen Benton was. There was a message before they left Paris. She was planning to meet them in Switzerland. Helen was quite worried. Was the message really from Karen?

Everyone in the bus was trying to sleep. Everyone except Helen. She started to write in her diary.

Paris, August 16th

Paris was fun. We visited Versailles and I remembered all the history about Marie Antoinette. I felt very proud of myself! I've decided that I like this job very much.

We enjoyed ourselves walking down the Champs Elysées and visiting Montmartre. Angela had a headache in the afternoon and so she went back to the hotel. We were all happy about that. But what about Vic? Well, I was surprised. He sat with Bill and Maisie and me in a café in one of the little streets in Montmartre and he told us funny stories about his travels. We all laughed a lot. Bill and Maisie were very interested in Eastern Europe. I realized then that I do like Vic.

He seems different when he isn't with Angela. He was very nice. But I'm going to be careful. I must remember what Lisa said: 'You always choose the wrong man . . . proud men . . . men with secrets.' Is Vic proud?

'So where's Karen?' Helen thought as they drove into Switzerland. She remembered what Mrs Jones in Penarth said about danger. 'I'm getting silly,' she thought. 'Perhaps my moon's in Scorpio or something.'

She decided to have a look at the special astrology chart. She looked around first at the others. Mary Foxley was reading a guide book. Angela James was sleeping with her mouth open.

'Not very pretty,' Helen thought.

Vic was reading a French newspaper. Sarah was talking about art to Tony. Bill Berryman was asleep.

'He *is* making some strange noises!' Helen thought.

She got her astrology chart out of her bag and began to study it. There were blue lines on it that went through different countries. The word 'Jupiter' was above one of the lines.

Yes, she remembered Lisa's words. That was her Jupiter line. It showed a place or a country where she could hope for good luck. She saw another line with 'Venus' written above it.

'What's that?' It was Vic. He came and sat next to her.

'Oh, nothing – just a map.' Helen put it away. She didn't want him to see it. 'Can't you sleep?'

'No. I don't need very much sleep. Four hours a night is enough for anyone. Now, Helen, where did you learn to speak French so beautifully?'

Helen went red and then began to tell him about her studies at university. She loved French and Italian art. But very soon she felt that she was talking too much. Men always liked to talk, she remembered. 'What about you? What do you do?' she asked.

'A bit of this and a bit of that. I love history and I love art. That's why I like travelling around Europe. I enjoy visiting different cities. I photograph old buildings – palaces, bridges, churches, that kind of thing.'

'So you're a photographer? That's why your camera case is so big?'

'Er – yes – I send my photographs to a company and they sell them to different magazines. American ones.'

'What's your favourite country?'

'Out of all of them? Austria, perhaps. I love the snow and the mountains. Climbing's my favourite sport. But I think the painted churches of Romania are very interesting, don't you?'

'Please tell me about them. You clearly know a lot.'

Helen knew about them too, but she didn't tell him this. She always did that with men. 'Maybe I should try to change,' she thought. Suddenly she wanted to sleep, but this was her job and he was an interesting man. She wanted to be friendly with him. But not too friendly, she thought. She was the tour guide.

He smiled at her. Then he took out his photographs and began to describe the churches. Helen smiled back.

Chapter 8   In Basle

Hotel du Parc, Basle, August 17th
Dear Diary,

It's midnight. We've travelled without stopping from Paris. I'm very tired, but I've had another look at my chart. My Jupiter line goes through the east coast of Australia. That means I'll have good luck there. Perhaps I'll write and tell Tom about that. It's strange. I haven't thought about him very much on the trip, but I still miss him.

My Venus line looks good. It goes through the middle of Italy. That means love in Italy. Will it be an Italian, or someone on the bus?

I'm getting more interested in Vic, but I don't understand. Why does he want to come on a tour like this? He already knows Europe better than I do. He's visited Paris many times before. Also, when we were leaving France, he began to act very differently. I don't know how exactly. He was just – strange. He spent a lot of time putting his photographs away and getting out his passport. He's not usually so careful.

When we arrived in Switzerland, he seemed OK again. He and some friends are starting a travel company. He asked me to work for them. I can choose the tours that I do. He offered me more money than Global Tours. 'It's the chance of a lifetime,' he said.

Perhaps he came on this tour to learn more about the travel business and about tours like these.

So, we're in Lucerne tomorrow. Then after that is Venice. I have to read all about the Doge's Palace. I need to remember when it was built. I'll also have to tell people some of the things that happened in it.

This job is harder than I thought. But I love it, even with people like Angela James on the tour!

Chapter 9   Karen Arrives

'Are you Helen?'

Helen turned. In front of her was a short woman with brown hair.

'Yes, I am.'

'I'm Karen Benton. I've only just arrived in Lucerne. I was worried about finding you. But you have 'Global Tours' written all over your bags. I couldn't miss you!'

Karen was a happy-looking woman and Helen liked her.

Mary Foxley came towards them. Helen introduced her to Karen.

'The others will be down soon,' Mary said to Karen. 'We're all going on a boat trip on the lake. Are you coming?'

'Sure. I'm sorry I'm so late.'

'What was the problem?' Helen asked.

'My passport was stolen, and some other things too.'

'Oh, no! That's terrible,' said Mary.

'What did you do?' asked Helen.

'I went to the police in Copenhagen. That's where my bag was stolen. A lot of passports are disappearing, they said. There are a lot of criminals in Europe doing this. The police can't do much.'

'What do the thieves do with the passports?' Helen was interested.

'They take out the photographs and put new ones in. People buy them to become a different person. It's easy, they said.'

'So have you got a passport now?'

'Yes. It took a long time, but I got one. So here I am.'

'We're happy you've come.'

'Thank you. Whose room am I in?' Karen looked around. Mary looked at Helen.

'Angela James. She's over there.' Helen pointed to Angela. 'She's wearing purple shorts and a yellow T-shirt.'

'The one talking to the man with a beard?' asked Karen.

'That's right. She can be difficult at times . . . ' Helen began.

'I'm sure I won't have any problems,' Karen said. 'I'll go and talk to her.'

Helen was surprised. Karen walked over to Angela and put out her hand. In a few minutes they were laughing together.

'I don't understand,' Helen said.

'What don't you understand?' Vic asked. He was standing quietly behind her.

'Oh, hi! Well, it's my job to help everyone on this trip to be happy. But when I talk to Angela, she always looks angry or bored. Now look at her. She's laughing with a person that she's only just met. She never does that with me. I think she hates me!'

'That's *her* problem, Helen. All the others think you're an excellent tour guide! I know they do. That's why I want you to work for my company.'

Helen went red. 'Thanks, Vic,' she said.

'You're welcome,' he said. 'Now, I'll go and introduce myself to Karen.'

'What's this about a job?' Mary Foxley asked.

'Pardon?' Helen turned and looked at her. She didn't know that Mary was near them. Perhaps she wanted to ask Vic something.

'Oh, it isn't my business. I'm sorry,' Mary said.

'No. It's not a secret. Or I don't think it is. Vic has a travel company and . . . ' Helen told Mary about his job offer.

'Oh, I see.'

Mary took off her glasses and looked away. Just then, Helen noticed something. There was a strange look in Mary's eyes. She seemed a different person.

'Do you know anything about Vic's company, Mary?'

'No, nothing. I'm so sorry. It really isn't my business.' Mary put her glasses on again. Suddenly she was the quite ordinary secretary that nobody wanted to talk to.

Chapter 10 An Accident at the Lake

'Did you get some good pictures of the mountains, Bill?'

'Yes, thanks, Vic. We have mountains in Colorado, of course, but the friends back home love to see videos of Europe.'

They were on Lake Lucerne. Vic and Bill Berryman were standing on the top part of the boat, looking up at the mountains. The sky was bright blue and the water was clear.

'I took some good photographs of these mountains last year. *International Geographic* bought them from me. They thought they were perfect.'

'That's great, Vic. Just great. Maybe you can give me some lessons.'

Vic smiled at him. 'Videos are different from real photographs, Bill. I haven't got time to teach you about taking pictures. It's an art. And I'm on holiday.'

'Oh, sure. I didn't mean . . . '

'For example, when I've got a headache, I don't ask you for medicine. You're on holiday. I think I'll go and talk to Angela.'

Helen didn't mean to hear this, but she was sitting round the corner, out of the wind. How strange! Was this the same Vic who told them funny stories in Montmartre? Was it the same Vic who told her to believe in herself? This Vic didn't seem to be the same man. He was quite rude to the American doctor. She shook her head. What was happening?

'We're back. Come on, everyone. Let's get off,' Noel shouted.

Helen was still on the top part of the boat. She looked down and saw Mary Foxley walking slowly off the boat. Sarah was behind her. Karen Benton was in front.

Suddenly, Mary fell.

'Mary, be careful!' Helen shouted. But Mary was already in the water.

Angela James screamed. Jean Summers pushed Sarah out of the way and jumped into the lake. Someone shouted, and Angela screamed again. Helen ran down the stairs.

'Excuse me! I'm the tour guide, I must help!' she shouted at the people who were crowding around.

She got to the big 'Exit' sign and looked down between the boat and the land. Karen was pulling Mary out of the water. Jean was still in the water, pushing Mary from the other side.

Helen ran off the boat. 'What can I do?' she asked.

Jean got out of the water and sat next to Mary. Karen was helping to dry Mary with a towel.

Mary opened her eyes. 'I'm all right, really,' she said.

'Come on. Let's get her to the hotel and out of those wet clothes,' Karen suggested.

'Find Bill first. He's a doctor. He must have a look at her,' Jean said.

Helen looked around and saw Bill Berryman in his yellow shirt and pink shorts. He was just getting off the boat.

'Bill! Mary fell in the water. Can you come and look at her? Is she all right?' she asked.

Bill didn't seem very interested. 'She looks OK. Just put her to bed,' he said, without even coming very close. He was carrying his video camera. 'I got some fine pictures of the lake. I must see them now,' he said. He began to walk towards the hotel.

Helen looked at him. She, Karen and Jean started to help Mary back to the hotel.

'I can walk back to the hotel. Just find my glasses for me,' Mary said.

Helen went back to look for them. Vic came up to her with the glasses in his hand.

'Are you looking for these?' he asked Helen.

She thanked him. 'I can't understand how that happened,' she told him.

'No. Perhaps she needs stronger glasses.' Vic smiled as he said this, but only with his mouth. There was a cold, hard look in his eyes.

'I'll give these to her,' Helen said, pointing to the glasses. 'Can you look after the group for me, Vic?'

'Sure. No problem,' Vic answered with the same cold smile.

Helen didn't really have time to think about it all. She ran after Mary, Jean and Karen.

Venice, August 21st
Dear Diary,

I'm finding some of the group very difficult! The biggest problem is Angela. She always seems to be angry. When I talk to Vic, it gets worse. Her face changes and her mouth becomes even smaller and tighter. Not a nice woman!

And there's Mary. When we stop somewhere, she always buys postcards and stamps, or presents for this person and that person in the office. Perhaps she wants to show us all that she has friends, somewhere. She's always writing postcards and then looking for post boxes. I must try to find something about her that I like. I did feel very sorry for her when she fell in the lake. She was very brave.

Bill Berryman was useless when the accident happened. Useless. And he calls himself a doctor. He was only interested in his video. Selfish man! Does Maisie really love him? Perhaps she doesn't. Why do they both wear those brightly-coloured clothes all the time? Bill's legs are so thin and hairy. And why does she always agree with him? Is she being a 'good wife'? I think it's boring.

Noel, Martin and Richard ('the three boys') are fun, but they're too young for me. They're still at university. But Sarah seems to like them very much. Perhaps she's trying to be twenty again. It's strange that she and Vic aren't friendly. She sells old furniture, but she seems more like an artist. I've never seen her talking to Vic.

I really can't understand Vic. He can be very friendly, but why was he so rude to Bill on the boat? And then, last night, we arrived in Venice and went around the city in a gondola. It was so romantic! We had a wonderful dinner and then Vic started to argue with Noel and Martin about money. The meal seemed quite cheap. But Vic decided to argue.

'You had the most expensive food on the menu,' he said to Noel. 'I had the cheapest. I don't understand why I have to pay for you.' Then he got up, threw some money on the table and left.

I couldn't believe it. He was so rude. The meal was excellent and it wasn't expensive.

Everyone was quiet. I felt terrible, but I had to do something. I decided to pay Vic's full amount out of the money from Global Tours and to see him about it later.

I went to his room when we got back. He wasn't there, so I'll have to see him about it in the morning. I hate arguments. But it's my job.

Chapter 11   From Venice to Rome

Helen knocked at Vic's door. There was no answer. She walked downstairs, pushed through the hotel doors and went out into the narrow street.

'Helen!' She turned. Vic was walking towards her. He was smiling and waving to her. 'Come for breakfast with me. Let's go to St Mark's Square and hide from the others.'

'Vic, I need to talk to you.'

He took her arm and started to walk with her towards the square. Part of her wanted to go, but she stopped. She took her arm away.

'Vic, I can't have breakfast in St Mark's. You know I have to be at the hotel with the group.'

'Oh, of course. You're the tour guide. I'm sorry.'

'Don't be silly. You know it's my job. And breakfast at St Mark's is very expensive. We've paid for breakfast at the hotel and last night you didn't pay enough for your dinner.'

'Ah. You're angry with me. I'm so sorry.' Vic smiled at her.

Helen looked at him. There was something about him that she didn't like.

'Where did you go last night? I went to your room this morning and you weren't there.'

A strange look came over Vic's face. Then it disappeared. He laughed.

'No. It isn't my business. I'm sorry,' Helen said quickly.

'It's OK. I have some friends in Venice. I decided to go and see them. That's all. Sometimes I get bored with the group.

'Well, I had to pay your part of the bill last night.'

'I'll give it to you, Helen. Please excuse me. It's probably Mars on my Gemini.'

Helen looked at him in surprise. Was he laughing at her? Did he know she believed in astrology? How did he know?

'Let's go and have breakfast with them. I'll say sorry and then all will be well,' Vic said.

Helen didn't feel comfortable. What did Lisa say about men with secrets?

'Are we going to the Doge's Palace this morning?'

'Yes, and the Lido★ in the afternoon.'

★ Lido: one of the islands of Venice.

'Wonderful. It will be very hot. Just perfect for a swim.'

Florence, August 24th
Dear Diary,

Well, we've been in Italy five days now and – nothing. When I say 'nothing', I mean no love. The young men wave and shout 'bellissima★', but nothing real. Vic decided not to come to the Uffizi. He's not very interested in the paintings there, he said. Strange. Doesn't he love all Italian art? He went off alone. He wanted to visit one of the hill towns, perhaps San Gimignano. I wanted to go with him to drink the famous white wine. But I had to take the group around Florence. It was a strange day really.

As always, I loved the Uffizi. But Mary didn't stay long. Her feet were hurting her and she went back to the hotel. She loves Italian art, too. Bill and Maisie Berryman looked bored. Maisie wanted to go shopping. Bill was still using his video camera.'

Noel and the boys wanted to talk to the Italian girls and eat ice cream. I tried to make the paintings interesting for them, but they left early. Probably for a drink.

Angela didn't even look at Botticelli's painting, The Birth of Venus. She was very tired. I really don't know what Vic and she can talk about.

Sarah wanted to visit some of the churches. She really prefers Eastern European buildings. She and Vic have similar interests, but she never talks to him. And she doesn't talk to me very much. She's a bit of a mystery.

I sent a postcard to Tom. I probably won't know anything about him until I get back to the UK. Anything can happen before that.

Tomorrow we're leaving Florence for Rome. A beautiful city! The City of Dreams! Perhaps Venus will work in Rome.

◆

★ bellissima: the Italian word for *very beautiful.*

They were standing in the middle of the Via Veneto★. The sun was very hot and it was time for lunch.

'OK, everyone. This is your free afternoon in Rome,' Helen told the group.

'I think Maisie and I will go to the Colosseum†. We want to make this video really interesting for the people back home.'

'That's great, Bill. Have fun. And what are you going to do, Angela?' Helen tried to smile.

Angela looked at her. Helen didn't like her look, but she continued to smile.

'Me? I'm going back to the Vatican Museum. You took us around it too quickly this morning, Helen. I need more time. Coming, Vic?'

Angela walked off. Vic looked quickly at Helen and followed her.

Helen felt angry. Angela was always quite rude, but that was *very* rude. And now she was with Vic. Helen wanted him to take her somewhere for the afternoon.

He sat next to her on the bus all the way from Florence to Rome. But while she and Vic were trying to talk, Angela was shouting questions. What was the population of Rome? How many hills was Rome built on? Silly questions. Angela was like a child, Helen decided. She refused to play her games.

Just before they arrived in Rome, Helen told Vic about Tom.

Vic looked deep into her eyes. 'You must forget the past. Look to the future,' he told her.

'He's interested in me,' she thought.

Now he was with Angela. Sometimes life isn't easy. She turned back to talk to the group.

Nobody was there. She saw Mary Foxley disappearing down

★ Via Veneto: a famous street in Rome.

† Colosseum: a very old building in Rome.

the street. Helen suddenly felt quite lonely. She decided to walk along the Via Veneto.

It was very hot, but there were a lot of tourists walking around, even at three o'clock in the afternoon. A waiter called to Helen. 'Signorina*!'

'Caffe con latte, per favore[†],' said Helen as she sat down.

'Ah! You speak good Italian,' said a man at the table next to hers. 'Can I join you?'

Helen was feeling lonely. She was also angry that she was not in love yet. Her Venus line went through Italy. Where was love? Perhaps it was here. Now.

'Please do,' she replied.

He was about thirty, she guessed. His hair was dark, and he was dressed beautifully. He wore a light grey suit and a pale pink shirt. 'A businessman,' thought Helen. 'He's different from Vic. Forget Vic. Forget Tom. I'll enjoy myself. Venus is working.'

'What is your name? Tell me about yourself. You are a very lovely woman.' He took her hand and kissed it.

Rome, August 27th

Oh, Diary, I was a little stupid this afternoon. No, very stupid. That's what loneliness can do. Why did I spend the afternoon with Mario? Why didn't I read my book, or take more photographs? Well, Mario practised his English and we did laugh a lot. He said nice things about my hair and eyes. I loved it all. This was Venus!

So I imagined that this was love in Rome! We drank some wine and he invited me for dinner. I told him my plans for the evening, with the group. But just then, a little boy came running up to him.

Mario tried to push him away. 'He's asking for money,' he said. He forgot that I speak Italian perfectly.

---

* Signorina: an Italian word that describes an unmarried woman.
[†] Caffe con latte, per favore: *Coffee with milk, please,* in Italian.

'Come home, Papa,' the boy said as he pulled at his arm. *'Mama's waiting for you. Everyone's waiting for you. Let's go home for the party, Papa.'* It was his wife's birthday party.

I was so angry. On his wife's birthday, he was sitting in a café on the Via Veneto with another woman. And he wanted me to go to dinner with him! Men!

I'm tired of men. That's it now. The end. Tom is probably having a great time in Australia. Let's just forget about him. Vic shows some interest and suddenly goes off with Angela. I can't understand what game he's playing. Then a married man invites me out when his wife is having a birthday party. Venus in Italy? No! I promise I'm not going to think about anything except my job for a very long time.

Chapter 12   On the Road Again

'Well, are you all ready to leave?' Helen asked the group. 'We've got to get to Brindisi to catch the boat to Greece this evening. It will be beautiful sailing down the Adriatic coast tomorrow morning.'

'I'd like to post some cards before we leave Italy, Helen.'

'Fine, Mary, I'm sure that will be possible.'

Helen took a long, deep breath. She was feeling very tired. This job was very hard work. She felt like their mother. 'When people aren't falling in lakes, they're arguing about money. And when they aren't doing that, they want to post postcards. When will I get a rest?' she thought.

'Feeling tired, Helen?'

Vic looked serious. Helen wanted to believe that he really was worried about her. His eyes looked deep into hers.

'No. I'm fine, thank you,' she said quickly. 'It will be wonderful to see Greece and Turkey.'

'Yes. Both places are very special for me.'

'Are they? I thought Italy was going to be special for me. But . . .' Helen stopped herself. She refused to talk about herself to him again.

She looked up, but he was walking to the back of the bus with the boys. 'What's the matter with him?' Helen thought. 'I can't understand him. Sometimes he seems interested in me and at other times he doesn't. He often goes for walks alone at night. Sometimes he joins in with everything that we're doing. At other times nobody knows where he is. He's a mystery.'

Helen began to dream a little. In her dream, he took her to the hills in the evening and said 'I love you'. But did she really want him?

Chapter 13 From Italy to Greece

They were crossing the Adriatic from Italy to Greece by boat. Sarah Lawrence was lying on the top part of the ship. She was wearing a red swimsuit and was covering herself with oil. Bill Berryman stopped videoing. The sun was bad for her, he told her. Sarah didn't seem to be listening. Bill's wife, Maisie, was reading a book. Helen could see the cover. A tall, dark Italian-looking man was kissing a young woman who looked Scandinavian. 'A Week in Rome' was the title.

Helen looked away. She didn't want to think about love – in Rome or any other place. Then she saw Angela. She was looking bored as usual. She was walking to the side of the ship. There was a large plastic bag in her hand. It was full.

'Angela! No!' someone shouted. It was Noel, one of 'the boys'.

'What's the problem?'

'Don't throw that in the sea!' Noel told her.

'Oh, no!' Helen thought. 'Why does Angela always do the wrong things? Now there'll be an argument.'

Angela dropped the bag over the side and then turned to Noel. She smiled.

'Really? Tell me about it.'

Noel went red but didn't answer.

'She's angry with me because I didn't talk to her on the bus down to Brindisi,' Vic said very quietly to Helen.

Helen looked round in surprise. She didn't know Vic was there. 'Oh, Angela's always angry. I don't even notice now.'

Vic smiled. 'You're a very intelligent woman, Helen.' Helen smiled politely. She didn't want to have any quiet talks with Vic again. 'I just wanted to ask you something, Helen. Can you put a package in your case for me before we leave the boat? And give it back to me in Athens?'

Helen was surprised again. What was this about?

'I don't understand,' she said. 'Why can't *you* take it to Athens?'

'I haven't got enough room for it in my case. It's a present for a friend of mine in Athens and I just thought . . . '

Helen didn't feel very comfortable with this, but she smiled back at him.

'I'm afraid my case is full already, Vic. You know I have so many papers. Why don't you ask Angela? Her case is big – very big. I'm sure that she'll take it. If you ask her nicely!'

Vic looked hard at her and then laughed. 'Of course! Angela. She'll do it.'

Helen looked at him as he climbed the steps up to the top part of the ship.

'He spends a lot of time with Angela. She can help him. Hmm. What can be in the package?' she thought.

♦

There was a letter waiting for her in Patras, their first stop in Greece. It was from Jill. She opened it when they got back on the bus again.

Dear Helen,

How are you? I hope the people on your tour are interesting. I hope you're enjoying the tour, too.

I'm writing this because I have some very good news. I've just finished my course. And I've got a job, too! I'm going to Papua New Guinea to study the trees there. I'll be there for two years.

I'm flying to Australia first. I'll be in Sydney for three days before I go to New Guinea. We have to change planes in Brisbane. Imagine! Isn't that where Tom is now? I can phone his mother and get his number. I'll phone him while I'm there.

Have you still got the plate?

Love,
Jill

Helen looked out of the window. There were olive trees on the hills, and the ground was yellow and rocky. Goats were moving around under the trees.

'The goats are looking for something to eat,' thought Helen. 'Goats will eat anything. Oh, home seems so far away. And Tom, too. Maybe he's got my postcard from Paris now.'

Suddenly, the bus stopped. Ben got out. Then he shouted to Helen, 'I think we've got a problem!'

Helen got out, too. She could see clouds of smoke.

'Where's that coming from?'

'I think the engine's too hot. Has anyone got any water?'

Tony, Jean's husband, came out.

'I'll walk to the nearest village and get some.'

'Thanks, Tony,' Helen said, 'but perhaps the nearest village is twenty kilometres away.'

'That's all right, Helen,' Tony answered. He took some empty bottles and began walking back along the road.

Helen got back into the bus and explained the problem calmly. Bill Berryman woke up.

'What's the matter? Why aren't we moving?'

Angela looked angry, closed her eyes and seemed to go to sleep.

'Is there a coffee shop anywhere around here?' Maisie asked.

'Helen, is there a shop here that sells—' Mary Foxley began.

'Postcards? No, Mary. There'll be some in Athens.'

Angela suddenly opened her eyes. 'How long will we be here?' she asked.

'I'm afraid I don't know.'

Angela looked even angrier and closed her eyes again.

Helen got out of the bus and stood on the road. Ben and Stan were looking at the engine.

'You chose the wrong person to be angry with,' a voice behind her said.

She turned. 'Yes, I did, didn't I, Vic?'

He smiled, but again only with his mouth and not with his eyes.

'I think I'll have a look at the view,' he said.

Helen watched him as he walked away. She had a very different idea of him since their arrival in Greece. He only did what he wanted to do. He only spoke to her when he wanted something from her. When she wanted some help from him, he was tired. When she wanted to talk about something, he wanted to be alone.

Then she remembered something strange. On the way to Brindisi he told her about his swim in Ostia★ after a visit to the

---

★ Ostia: a town on the coast near Rome.

Vatican Museum with Angela. But Bill saw him walking near the Colosseum. 'Why did he lie?' she thought.

Helen got back into the bus and spoke to the others.

'I'm sorry about this, everyone. I'm sure it won't take long.'

August 30th, 11.45 p.m., on the bus
Dear Diary,

Perhaps my Uranus line goes through Greece. I've decided that Uranus means trouble and sudden change.

Tony was gone for hours before he came back with some water. Then we had to find a garage. But the bus is OK now – I hope! It's almost midnight and we still haven't arrived in Athens. Angela is angry with me now because I don't speak Greek. And because of the problems with the bus. Do I have to be perfect? I think I'll look for a different job after this trip. I've always wanted to go to Africa. Perhaps I can find a job in Kenya. Maybe I can work with wild animals. Or perhaps I'll travel around Australia and see Tom. Dreams! All dreams!

Chapter 14   An Evening at the Theatre

On their first morning in Athens, Helen took her films to a shop next to the hotel. The next day, the photos were ready. She began looking through them. They were from Rome, and they were of everyone in the group. Nobody knew she was taking photographs of them. She wanted to keep the photos for a surprise and then show them to everybody at the end of the tour.

One of the pictures was of Mary. She was talking to a strange-looking man in St Peter's Square. The man in the picture was dark, with a moustache. To Helen, Mary seemed to know him well. In the photo Mary looked quite different as she talked to him. There was the same intelligent look that she noticed once before. Mary almost looked like a different person.

There was also a photo of Maisie and Bill Berryman with their mouths open, trying to eat very large ice creams in a street cafe. They looked very funny.

And the photo of Vic . . . that was strange. That was the afternoon when Bill saw him at the Colosseum. She saw him too – near the Via Veneto at about five o'clock. He was talking to – guess who? – Sarah! They looked very friendly. 'But I've never seen them talking before or since then,' Helen thought. She looked at the photograph more carefully. Was Vic giving Sarah something? What was it?

She noticed another thing in the photograph. A man with a dark moustache was standing behind Vic and Sarah. She looked back at the photograph of Mary and the man in St Peter's Square. It was the same man!

She put the photographs down.

'Well,' she thought, 'I don't know who's doing what! But this evening we're going to the Herod Atticus Theatre, under the Acropolis*, and we're going to see some Greek dancing.'

♦

The lights were on around the Acropolis. They lit up the old walls and the olive trees on the hill. Lots of people were walking around and enjoying the lights of Athens and Piraeus below them.

'Just imagine,' said Maisie to Vic. 'People have walked over these stones for thousands of years. Isn't that wonderful?'

'Really and truly wonderful,' Vic said coldly.

Helen pulled Vic away. 'Please be more polite to her.'

'Why? She's so stupid.'

Helen took a deep breath. 'Vic . . . '

'You're great, Helen. You've changed since we began this holiday. At the beginning you were a quiet little girl from Penarth. You couldn't tell anyone what to do. And now . . . '

'Tickets, please. Tickets.' The man on the gate put out his hand to Sarah.

'That woman in the blue dress has got our tickets.' Sarah pointed to Helen.

'Tickets, please.'

---

* Acropolis: a famous hill in Athens. There is a beautiful old building, the Parthenon, on the top of it.

Helen searched in her bag. She couldn't find the tickets. Where were they?

Helen felt terrible. 'Did I leave them in the hotel?' she thought. 'The dancing begins in five minutes.' She could see the girls and boys in their beautiful clothes. What could she do? She looked again in every part of her bag. No, they weren't there.

She turned to the group. 'I'm sorry. I can't find the tickets.'

'Helen, this really isn't good enough.' Vic was smiling. He was enjoying himself.

She was very angry with him. She suddenly saw the worst side of Vic. 'He enjoys it when people are in difficulty. Why haven't I noticed it before?' she asked herself.

Helen walked over to the man at the gate and smiled at him.

'I'm very sorry. I've searched for our tickets and I can't find them. I *did* have them. I bought them yesterday in Athens. Please let us in.'

'*Endaxi. Endaxi*★. There are lots of seats over there. Just take your friends and sit down. Enjoy the dancing. We will play a special song for you. You are a very beautiful woman.'

Helen laughed. She felt better. 'I'll love the Greeks for the rest of my life,' she thought.

'Helen, you're wonderful.' Karen sat next to her and offered her some chocolates. 'You're the best tour guide.'

Helen was really surprised. She felt good about herself. She sat in her seat, ate a chocolate and started to enjoy the dancing. Vic tried to speak to her but she pretended not to hear him.

The evening was great. The girls and boys sang, and their dancing was wonderful and fast. Everyone enjoyed themselves. At the end a man came out to the front and sang a quiet, beautiful song to Helen. It was a perfect night.

★ Endaxi: The Greek word for OK.

September 2nd
Dear Diary,

After the dancing, some people invited us to dinner! We went to a restaurant in the Plaka and danced until 3 a.m. It was great fun. We all threw plates and danced on the tables.

I'm tired now but tomorrow – no, today – we're going to Istanbul. Another long ride. I hope everyone goes to sleep! We've seen so much of Greece. It's very beautiful and the people are so friendly. I really love it.

Chapter 15 Istanbul

It was evening, almost night, as the bus drove into Istanbul. Europe and Asia met there.

'This is the last stop,' thought Helen. 'Soon they'll all fly back to London.'

She looked around the bus. Vic was talking quietly to Angela. She was laughing. It didn't worry Helen now. She decided that she really didn't like Vic very much. He still went off alone. He even went to different restaurants from the group sometimes. When he came with them, he was sometimes quite rude. But he never spoke to Sarah. She stayed with the three noisy students and laughed at their stupid jokes. She never talked to Helen.

'We can have a meal here at the hotel or go down by the water. What does everyone want to do?' Helen tried to sound interested, but she felt very tired after the long drive.

'What do *you* want to do?' Karen asked.

Helen was surprised. 'What do you mean?'

'Tell us what *you* want to do.'

'I want to have dinner here in the hotel and go to bed very early. I'm very tired. But . . . '

'Fine. Right, everyone. Helen's staying here. We can find restaurants ourselves.'

43

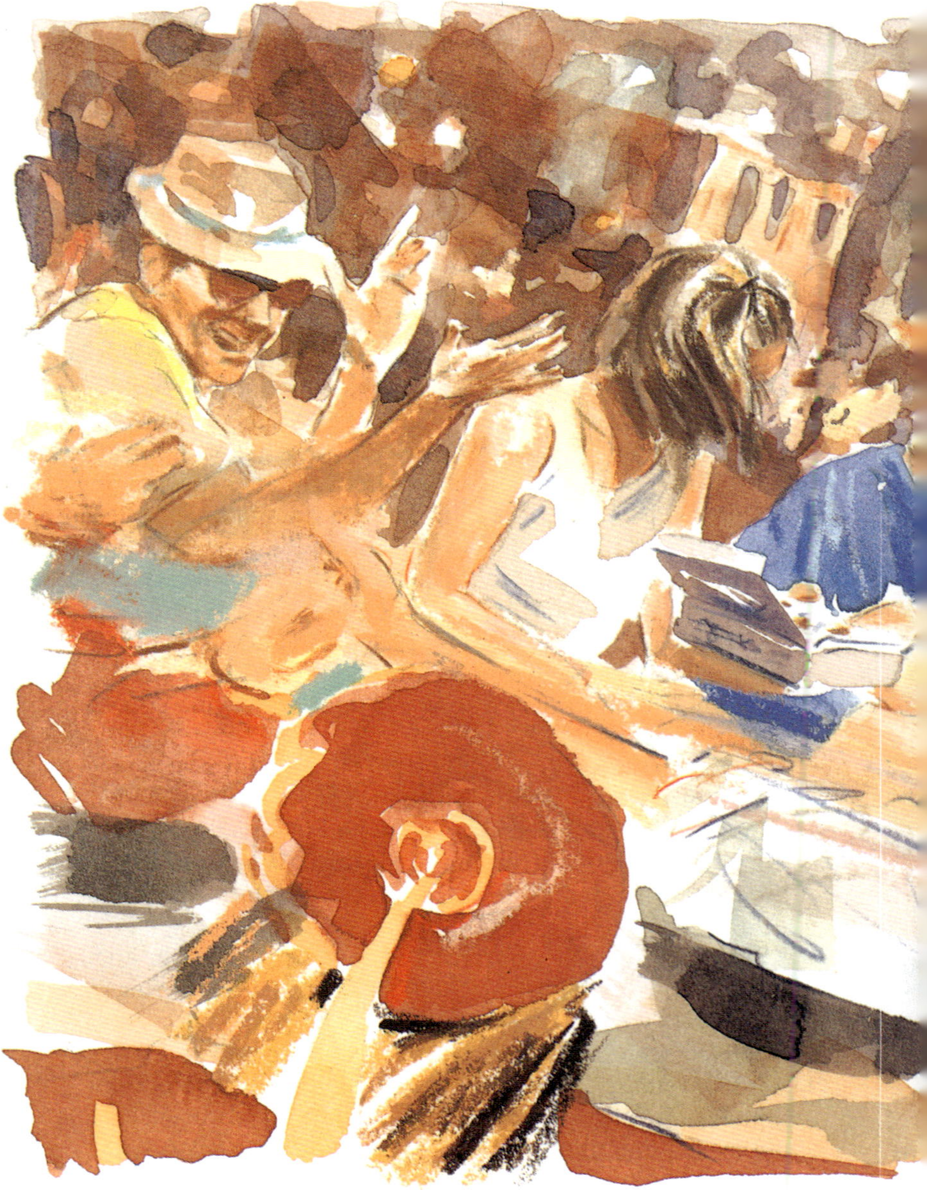

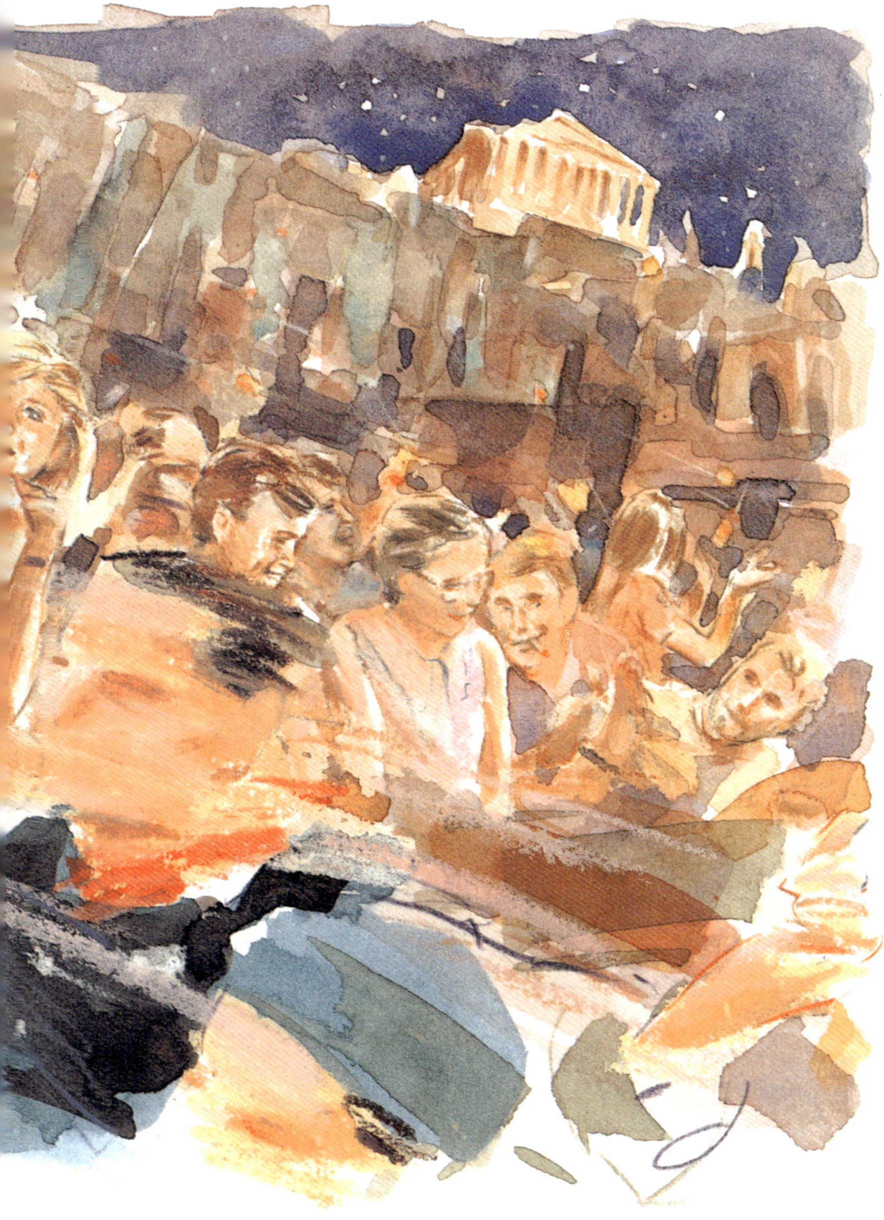

September 3rd
Dear Diary,

Karen was great this evening! I was too tired to be polite. We've got a full day tomorrow. First we're visiting Topkapi Palace and then we're going on the water, the Bosphorus. Turkey is a wonderful country and the people are so helpful. I love the art and the buildings. Perhaps I'll learn some Turkish, or . . .

I've just realized that I didn't write about Tom yesterday.
Perhaps I've stopped loving him.
Oh . . . I must go to sleep . . .

♦

'Can we go and see the Harem?' Mary asked Helen, as they all walked into Topkapi Palace.

Vic laughed. 'Why do you want to see where the sultan kept all his women, Mary?'

Mary looked down, took off her glasses and cleaned them. 'I – er–'

Helen turned to him angrily. But she spoke slowly and very quietly.

'The Harem is a very beautiful part of the palace. Mary is very interested in Turkish art, and many other people in the group are too. Go and see some different rooms if you want to.'

She looked straight into his eyes. Vic looked away and laughed.

'I usually prefer to walk around museums alone,' he said. 'I'll go and look at some plates.'

Vic walked off and immediately disappeared into the crowds.

There were a lot of visitors to the Topkapi that day. There were women from Arab countries in black dresses with small children running around. European tourists were taking lots of photographs. There were also some Turkish families on holiday, looking at their own history.

Helen counted the group. Ben and Stan, the two drivers, were shopping for their families in the city. Suddenly, Helen realized that Sarah wasn't there. She turned to the three boys.

'Where's Sarah? Have you seen her?'

'She *was* here, but she's left. She'll meet us all here at one o'clock.'

'Right. Let's look at the Harem first, shall we? Then perhaps the Islamic plates.'

'That sounds great to us, Helen. You're the boss.'

'I am,' said Helen and smiled. 'You're right.'

Two hours later, they were walking through a room full of Islamic bowls and plates when Helen saw Vic talking to a woman outside. Sarah? No, the woman was fat and had long fair hair. Helen walked to the door and looked out, but they were not there. As she turned back to look at some blue bowls, she saw Mary watching her. She looked different. There was something – well – she couldn't describe it.

'Do you think I can take a photograph of these bowls, Helen? I'd love to show them to my friends at my art class.'

'I'm sure you can buy some photographs in the shop, Mary.'

No, it was the same Mary, still interested in her postcards and her friends back home.

'I've got some photographs of you all in Rome,' Helen added. 'I think you'll laugh at them. It's nearly one o'clock. Shall we go and meet the others?'

'Fine. This has been wonderful – a really great visit, Helen,' said Tony.

'Great! I'm glad you liked it.'

'Well, I thought the Uffizi . . .' Angela started.

'Can I see the photographs that you took in Rome, Helen?'

Helen turned to see Mary next to her.

'Yes, of course I'll show them to you, Mary.'

Chapter 16   Holiday Photos

September 5th
Dear Diary,
   1 a.m. I've just got in from the party! The group decided to give me an end-of-tour dinner. We had the most wonderful dinner of seafood and fish. Then there was music and dancing. Vic danced with Angela most of the night. She seemed very happy! Sarah danced with the three boys, and I was asked to dance by a very handsome Turkish man. He seemed interested in staying with me all evening, but I learnt my lesson in Italy.
   There was a postcard at the hotel from my mother. She says that a letter from Brisbane will arrive soon. That's probably from Tom. What will it say? I really don't feel anything about it. Nothing.
   So today they are all shopping, and then late tomorrow night I'll take them to the airport and say goodbye to them. Ben and Stan are driving back. I'll finish all the business with the company here and fly back in two days. Oh, I'm tired! I know my Uranus line goes through Turkey, too, but everything is calm and quiet.

   Helen was tidying her room before the group arrived. They wanted to see Bill's video of the trip and Helen's photographs.
   There was a knock on the door. It was Mary.
   'Can I see your photos, Helen?'
   'Oh, yes. You can have a quick look before the others come.'
   'I've got the video, Helen. Can I come in?' Bill put his head around the door. 'I'd just like to look at it quickly before the others come. Can I?'
   'Yes, of course.' Helen heard a cry from Mary and turned.
   'Oh, they are funny, Helen. You're a good photographer.'
   'Thanks, Mary. Now let's see if there are some funny pictures of all of us on the video.'
   The first part of the video showed the group getting onto the bus in London. Then walking down the Champs Elysées eating

ice creams. Helen wasn't very interested in that part and she felt quite tired. Her eyes started to close.

Suddenly, she felt Mary jump next to her. She looked up. There was the boat on the waters of Lake Lucerne, and a moving hand.

'Oh, there's me in the lake!' said Mary in a strange voice.

The picture changed to Venice, and they were all laughing on the gondola. Noel and Martin were pretending to sing.

Then the camera moved quickly and it was difficult to see.

'Was that the Doge's Palace?' asked Mary.

'I think I was walking too quickly there,' Bill said.

Just then, Helen saw Vic in the video. He was standing by the corner of a building, and he was giving something to a tall man. She couldn't see what it was.

'Can I come in?' Sarah put her head around the door.

'Yes! There are some funny ones of you, Sarah. Come and see. I'll go back to the beginning,' said Bill.

September 7th
Dear Diary,

Vic didn't come to see Bill's video. I don't know where he went. Angela wants to be a film actor now. Sarah left half-way through it. I think she was bored. The video wasn't very interesting, but perhaps Bill's friends in the States will like it!

Later I'm taking them to the airport. Then I can have a rest. Well, nothing strange has happened in Turkey. Pluto means deep, dark secrets, but I haven't noticed anything. That letter from Tom hasn't come. Or perhaps it's from Jill. I try not to think about Tom now.

Chapter 17   At the Airport

'I really enjoyed it when the bus broke down in Greece.'

'I loved the beautiful plates in the Topkapi Museum.'

'Well, I'm glad that you all had a good time.'

'Helen, you were a wonderful tour guide. She was, wasn't she?'

'Yes, she was.' Vic came up and gave Helen a kiss. 'Thanks for everything.'

Helen looked at him. She knew now that Vic wasn't honest. He was proud, but he also told lies. He wasn't a good man. And there was another thing . . . What was it . . . ?

'Vic, tell me . . . Did you get your package to your friend?'

Vic picked up his large camera case and put it on his shoulder. 'Yes, thanks. Angela took it. Well, see you, Helen.'

'Bye, Vic.'

Helen looked back at him as he showed his passport and ticket. Yes, he was a strange man. 'He never offered me that job with his company again,' she thought.

The passport officer looked carefully at Vic and his passport. Helen saw him ask Vic a question. Vic answered, laughed and started to move away. The man called him back.

'That's strange,' thought Helen. She looked around the airport. Bill and Maisie were asking for no-smoking seats. Mary Foxley wasn't there. 'She's probably looking for some more postcards,' Helen thought.

Sarah was standing behind Vic. She was waiting to show her passport.

'This isn't your passport,' Helen heard the officer say loudly to Vic.

'Yes, it is. I'm Vic Watson. I look exactly like the man in the photo. That's me. Now, can I go through and catch my plane?'

'The number of this passport is the number of a passport that was stolen last year in Austria.'

'I think you've made a mistake. That's my passport. I'm British. I want to go and catch my plane.'

Helen was surprised. She started to go to Vic. There

was a line of people behind him. Sarah was looking frightened.

'What's happening here, Vic?' Bill shouted. 'We've got a plane to catch in London to New York.'

Vic turned to him. 'This stupid man thinks that I have a stolen passport. It's impossible. Helen, tell him.'

Just then, three policemen came running towards the passport desk.

'What's happening? What are they doing?' Karen asked. 'They've got guns!'

She saw Vic turn and say something to Sarah. He took something from his camera case and dropped his case on the floor. Sarah ran towards the exit and Vic turned to run after her. Helen saw that he had a gun in his hand. Vic turned and shot at the policemen. People screamed and fell on the floor or hid behind chairs and tables. There were more shots, more screams and then silence.

Helen looked around the airport. She saw two policemen standing over Vic. Was he hurt? Was he dead? Mary Foxley was holding Sarah. Sarah looked very frightened.

A policeman pulled Vic to his feet. He wasn't hurt.

'Your passport smuggling days are finished. You and your girlfriend are going to prison for a very long time.'

Helen couldn't believe what was happening. She knew she should do something. But she couldn't move.

Some detectives ran into the airport. One took Sarah from Mary Foxley. Mary walked over to Helen and the group.

'So,' said Helen, 'they were smuggling passports across Europe?'

'Yes,' said Mary. 'I found a packet of them in Sarah's case in our room. They were taking them to the different countries that we visited. Thank you for putting me in the same room as her. It was useful.'

'So who are you, Mary?' asked Helen.

'I work for Interpol.'

'You're a policewoman! A detective! I thought you were a secretary.'

Mary took off her glasses and smiled. She looked a completely different person.

'It was a useful story. I had to find out how they smuggled the stolen passports into the different countries. Vic hid them in his camera case. It was too big for just one camera. I followed him everywhere. I saw the people that he met. I watched the things that he did. I knew Sarah was his girlfriend. She pushed me into the lake. I saw that on the video. She knew I wasn't a secretary. I think she saw me looking in her case one day.'

'That was very dangerous for you!'

'Perhaps.'

'Why were you always looking for postcards?' asked Jean.

'The postcards were just a game. I was being Mary Foxley.'

'A game. That's what Vic was playing with me,' Helen said.

'But you didn't play. That made him angry. He wanted you to smuggle passports for him.'

'Me? Never!'

'Remember that he asked you to work for his company?'

'Yes.'

'He didn't ask you to be a smuggler, did he?'

Helen looked at her. 'No, he didn't,' she said quietly. 'But he asked me to take a package to Athens for him.'

'It was full of passports.'

'How do you know?'

'I went to Angela's room and found them.'

'Oh! He asked me and I did!' Angela screamed. 'I took them. Oh! I'm a criminal!'

'Don't be stupid, Angela. You didn't know. But think next time. Use your head – like Helen.'

Vic walked by and smiled at Helen. Two policemen were holding his arms.

Helen turned away. She couldn't look at him.

'It's time for your plane, everyone. Goodbye. Have a good journey.'

Chapter 18   Helen's Decision

September 9th
Dear Diary,

Well, it was an exciting trip. Mary told me about Vic and Sarah. When they disappeared, they were always meeting someone about the passports. Sarah told Vic not to bring any passports with them on the plane. But he decided to take some in his camera case. So he and Sarah will spend many years in prison in Turkey. I'm not sorry.

Another surprising thing happened at the airport. Angela came up to me and kissed me.

'Thank you for a great holiday, Helen. You're a wonderful woman.'
I think I was more surprised at that than I was about Vic and Sarah. Well, it was an interesting beginning to my career!

I'd love to come back to both Greece and Turkey. Everyone was so friendly to me.

I feel I've changed a lot in the last few weeks. I had to be nice to difficult people and work very hard. But I had fun too.

And what about men? Tom – who's Tom? Then there was Vic. I saw what he was. I feel stronger.

The last two weeks have been so exciting. But what will I do when I get back – to Penarth? Oh, no. I can't stay there after this!

◆

On her last evening in Istanbul, Helen found two letters when she went back to the hotel. The first one was from Australia. The second was from London. She opened the one from Australia first.

Dear Helen,

Why didn't I see you before I left? I'm so sorry. I realize I was selfish. I promise I won't be selfish again.

I've thought about you a lot in the last month. Now I know what a wonderful woman you are. I love you. My mother often phones me and tells me about you. Your life sounds very exciting, but I would like you to come to Brisbane. I can find you a job. I do miss you very much.

You know I love you, Helen. It just took me some time to see it. Please come.

All my love,
Tom

Helen sat on the bed in her room and read the letter again. Her stomach was turning over.

'He wants me to go to Brisbane. What shall I do?'

She opened the other letter. It was from Global Tours. '...Thank you for doing a wonderful job on your first trip ...'

She read it quickly, and then she saw the last few lines:

'We would like to offer you another job with Global Tours. We are adding to our holidays and we would like you to take a group to Kenya for three weeks.'

'Kenya! Wonderful!' Helen couldn't believe it. She really wanted to go to Kenya. There was something dreamy about the name. Now she could go.

'Oh, I have a difficult decision to make. I hate making decisions like this.'

Helen looked at the two letters. She placed them side by side. She remembered Lisa's words: 'You'll get your chance of a lifetime this year.'

'What is my "chance of a lifetime"? To go to Australia and be with Tom? Or to be a tour guide in Kenya for Global Tours?'

She looked out across the Bosphorus. Here was the chance of a lifetime. No – two chances. Which one should she take? Then she realized: 'I've found it. I believe in myself. I don't think my happiness depends on a man. That's what I believed before. That's past. Now – Tom or Kenya?'

Helen looked out across the city. The light was beginning to change from a light blue to a soft grey.

'Perhaps I need to talk to someone about this. But who? There's nobody. I have to decide for myself. I guess this is growing up.'

Helen picked up the plate from Jill and read its message: 'Be true to yourself.' She smiled.

'Wait a second,' she told herself. 'It isn't Tom *or* Kenya. It isn't one or the other. I can go and work in Kenya. And I can tell Tom that I'll come out for a holiday later. He can wait. I won't make any quick decisions. I can take my time. I can find out who I am. That's my chance of a lifetime!'

ACTIVITIES

Chapters 1–6

Before you read
1 Have you travelled around Europe? Which countries did you visit/would you like to visit? Why?
2 Find the words in *italics* in your dictionary. They are all in the story.
   a Discuss why these words are in these groups.
   – *astrology   chart   planet*
   – *career   independent   respect*
   b Discuss these questions.
   – When do you *breathe* deeply (or take deep *breaths*)?
   – This story is about a '*chance* of a lifetime'. What do you think this *chance* is? Think of possible ideas.
   – Why do people write a *diary*? Do they ever read it again?
   – What kind of *museum* do you enjoy? Why?

After you read
3 Who are these people? What are they like?
   a Tom
   b Jill
   c Vic Watson
   d Sarah Lawrence
   e Mary Foxley
   f Bill Berryman
4 Which people say the following sentences? Who are they speaking to? Where are they?
   a 'A big international company has offered me a job!'
   b 'Shall I go and look for a job near him?'
   c 'Life is more than marriage and children.'
   d 'You always choose the wrong man.'
   e 'Pick up my case, will you?'
   f 'We'll throw her in a lake in Versailles and teach her to be polite.'

Chapters 7–12

Before you read
5 What do you think is going to happen next? Give your reasons.
6 Find these words in your dictionary. Tell a short story, using the words.
   argue   gondola

After you read
7 How does each of these people feel about the other person? Give reasons for your opinions.
   a Helen and Tom   **c** Bill and Vic
   b Angela and Helen   **d** Helen and Vic
8 Work in pairs. Act out the conversation between Helen and Mario in the restaurant in Rome.
   Student A: You are Mario. Invite yourself to sit with Helen. Explain why the little boy is talking to you.
   Student B: You are Helen. Listen to Mario. How do you feel when the little boy comes to the table? Tell him.

Chapters 13–18

Before you read
9 How do you think the story will end? What will Helen do after the trip?
10 Find these words in your dictionary. Put them in the sentences below.
   depend   engine   goat   harem   olive   pretend
   smuggle   sultan
   a The . . . . . kept forty women in his . . . .
   b We have no cows, so we . . . . . on milk from our . . . .
   c People were . . . . . into the country in boxes of . . . .
   d He . . . . . that the car was fine. But I couldn't start the . . . .

After you read

11 What decision does Helen make at the end of the story? Is it the right decision? What do you think?

12 Work with another student. Decide who Student B will be.

Student A: You work for Global Tours. Phone one of the tourists after the holiday. Ask for his/her opinions of the trip and the tour guide. Will he/she go on another Global tour?

Student B: You are one of the tourists in the group. Answer the questions.

13 Where are these places? Can you remember?

- **a** the Louvre
- **b** St Mark's Square
- **c** the Vatican Museum
- **d** the Herod Atticus Theatre
- **e** Lake Lucerne
- **f** the Uffizi
- **g** the Colosseum
- **h** Topkapi Palace

Writing

14 Write a newspaper report about Vic Watson and his passport smuggling business. Describe how he was caught.

15 You are Helen. Write a letter to Tom from Istanbul. Tell him what you are going to do. Tell him how you feel.

16 You are Bill Berryman. You want to write some words to go with your video of the trip through Europe. Choose part of the video. Describe the places and the people that your friends will see.

17 Write a letter to the writers of this book. Tell them what you liked about *Chance of a Lifetime*. Tell them what you disliked.

Answers for the Activities in this book are published in our free resource packs for teachers, the Penguin Readers Factsheets, or available on a separate sheet. Please write to your local Pearson Education office or to: Marketing Department, Penguin Longman Publishing, 5 Bentinck Street, London W1M 5RN.